Your Vision Journal

by

Jada Williams

Copyright © 2021 by Jada Williams

All rights reserved. No part of this book may be reproduced in any form or by any electronic or mechanical means, including information storage and retrieval systems, without permission in writing from the author, except by reviewer or presenter, who may quote brief passages in a review or presentation.

ISBN 978-1-7365717-7-4

Printed and bound in the United States 2021

Published by Sula Too Publishing
Tampa, Florida
www.sulatoo.com/publishing

This Vision Journal Belongs To:

_____

"Faith is the starting point of all accumulation of Riches"
                                              -Napoleon Hill

Create the space for your Vision to
become your Reality
with accountibility
https://www.yapaccountabilitypartner.com

Love,

Jada Williams
Your Accountability Partner

Jada Williams

Reflection

Where are you now? Life is a journey! Ask yourself the questions reflecting over your past year from today's date. It's a beautiful thing to look in the rear view mirror. We are going to smile on all the positive and rewarding endevors, shine up and improve on what is needed and leave some things right where they are! Behind us! What are you YAPPEN about? From this day forth, we will be mindful of the conversations we entertain, our thoughts, and the energy around us. That, I strongly believe, is a major key to success. Pushing the needle forward works best when there is perfect harmony in one's life! Things happen; its magic when you are focused and on point!

What Worked Best..

I Needed More......

Your Accountability Journal

Mirror Me...

Personal Accomplishments..

Career Accomplishments..

I Learned..
Grateful For..

Looking Forward

The vision starts here. Create the space for your dreams to become your reality! Write your vision down. Shine up and improve YOU!

Burning Desire*
Faith *
Persistence*...
Personal Goal..
I Want to Start..
Grateful For..

Your Accountability Journal

Type of Person I want to Be...

I want to Learn...

I want to Let Go..

Health Goals..

Voided Check
Savings Account/ Money
Earned (Revenue)

21 Things to Do Before Year End

Let's take better care of ourselves!
We all want to live a successful, intentional, purposeful life. STOP - don't over think it; You don't have to go drill sargent serious, but this is a great area to create the space of defining YOU.
"If I Think it; I Can Do It!"

Your Accountability Journal

Self-care Reminders

Physical-

Emotional-

Spiritual-

Creative-

Financial-

Career/ entrepreneurial

Education/ Self Development-

Complete this section by writing out 2-3 phrases of your favorite motivational statements you like and or your overall goal for each category. Self Reminders + The peace and calmness behind why we do what we do! Perfect for those "Everything Sucks" Days

200 Things I Want In Life..

Take the time to sit with yourself and reflect on all things you want out of life. This exercise will help you open up your mind to what uniquely matters to you. Youv'e now created your list of life goals...FYI most people can't think past 75 things they genuinely want from LIfe.

200 Things I Want In Life..

Jada Williams

200 Things
I Want In Life..

Transition into your Inner Bad Ass

Goals Next 3 Months..
January-March

Goals Next 3 Months..
April-June

Now let's get it done! Start with your list of 22 things you must get done by the end of the year. Take one item at a time from your list and accomplish it! Your list of 22 things will lead to you marking off one of your 200 things you want out of life.... Getting it done!

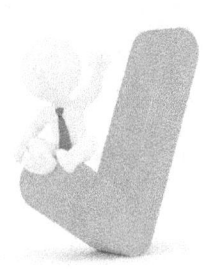

Goals Next 3 Months..
July - September

Goals Next 3 Months..
October - December

> "The wound is the place where the light enters you."
> —Rumi

Jada Williams

Your Accountability Journal

Jada Williams

Your Accountability Journal

Jada Williams

Your Accountability Journal

Jada Williams

Your Accountability Journal

Jada Williams

Your Accountability Journal

Jada Williams

Your Accountability Journal

What are you yappen about?
There are 4 types of conversations... Let's figure out how to stay out of some of them and thrive in the ones that matter most!

Types:
Conversation of Possibility - Explore alternatives
Conversation of Opportunity - Evaluate the good, the bad,
Coversation of Action - Duh take action, decision making
Conversation of BS - Stay far away when people have conversations and the objectives does not match; this causes frustration or a since of time be-ingwasted. Declare what type of conversation you are about to engage in and adjust accordingly. All things are not equal!
#positiveconversation #elevation

Your Accountability Journal

Jada Williams

"Visualization creates the space"

Jada Williams

Jada Williams

Your Accountability Journal

Jada Williams

Your Accountability Journal

Level up!..
Learn a new skill, trade, or hobby. Commonly expressed as Self developement is; Self Investment if you don't who will! This will also allow you to expand your circle, new exposures and experiences that often lead to mind blowing manifestations
Just Live and BE prepared for opportunity

Your Accountability Journal

"You've got to think high to rise"
Napoleon Hill

Jada Williams

Your Accountability Journal

Jada Williams

Your Accountability Journal

Jada Williams

"Our acts can be no wiser than our thoughts"

Your Accountability Journal

Glitter is always an option...
Yes know what makes you feel powerless.
Know what your weakness are. Also
know what makes you feel like a
superhero with all the power and talent
in the universe and focus most on that!
Master You

Your Accountability Journal

Jada Williams

Your Accountability Journal

Jada Williams

Your Accountability Journal

"I found the road to wealth when I decided that a part of all I earned was mine to keeep." George Clason

Own YOUR Glow...
Dress to feel confident not to impress!
Where what makes you feel good.

Your Accountability Journal

Jada Williams

Your Accountability Journal

Jada Williams

Your Accountability Journal

"Once you know who you are, you don't have to worry anymore." -Nikki Giovanni

Keep it 100 %...
What is your mission statement/ Motto?...Getting a PHD in Self will have you walking a little different. Some have said a pep in their step, or maybe even a glow to their look but its only accomplished by being true to you. Define who you are.

Your Accountability Journal

Jada Williams

Your Accountability Journal

Jada Williams

Your Accountability Journal

Jada Williams

Your Accountability Journal

"Know your strengths and use them often; build your future on you."

Know the business that pays you!
Be Consistent
Be Persistent
Be Engaged
Be Motivated
Be Flexible
Be Trainable
Be Authentically YOU

Your Accountability Journal

Jada Williams

Your Accountability Journal

Jada Williams

Jada Williams

"Turn your fears into your next accomplishments."

Your Accountability Journal

Money in the bank shorty what you think... Financial stability and confidence have a funny intanglement! sometimes better decision making happens when an individual is not financially stressed. Though life is not based on money we can agree we are all much happier when we're not robbing Peter to pay Paul.

Your Accountability Journal

Jada Williams

Your Accountability Journal

Jada Williams

Your Accountability Journal

Your Accountability Journal

Gratitude...

I am GRATEFUL
for..
Life...
Family...
Sunshine..
My
Mind..
Music..
Art..
Vision..
Soul..
Community..
Relationships..
Love..
Food & Medicince.. Butterflies &
Bees..

Gratitude...

Your Accountability Journal

Jada Williams

Your Accountability Journal

Jada Williams

Your Accountability Journal

"Remember why you started"

Jada Williams

Your Accountability Journal

Jada Williams

Your Accountability Journal

"The way to get started is to quit talking and start doing."

Your Accountability Journal

Creativity...
Be your own kind of BEAUTIFUL!
Use your imagination every day! I will forever be 27 years old. Why? I enjoyed that age. but reality is most people stop using their imagination in elementary school and mourf into dull or boring, complaining adults by the time they reach their freshman year in college. You have to be able to imagine it to

Your Accountability Journal

Jada Williams

Your Accountability Journal

Jada Williams

"Written down thoughts provide clarity"

Family
Friends
Community

Your Accountability Journal

Jada Williams

Jada Williams

Your Accountability Journal

Jada Williams

" Have the power to Let Go of;
focus on what is needed for your Achievements"

Your Accountability Journal

Jada Williams

Your Accountability Journal

Jada Williams

Your Accountability Journal

Jada Williams

Your Accountability Journal

Jada Williams

Your Accountability Journal

"Make your health a priority
Mind, Body & Soul"

Jada Williams

Your Accountability Journal

Jada Williams

Monthly Snap Shots..

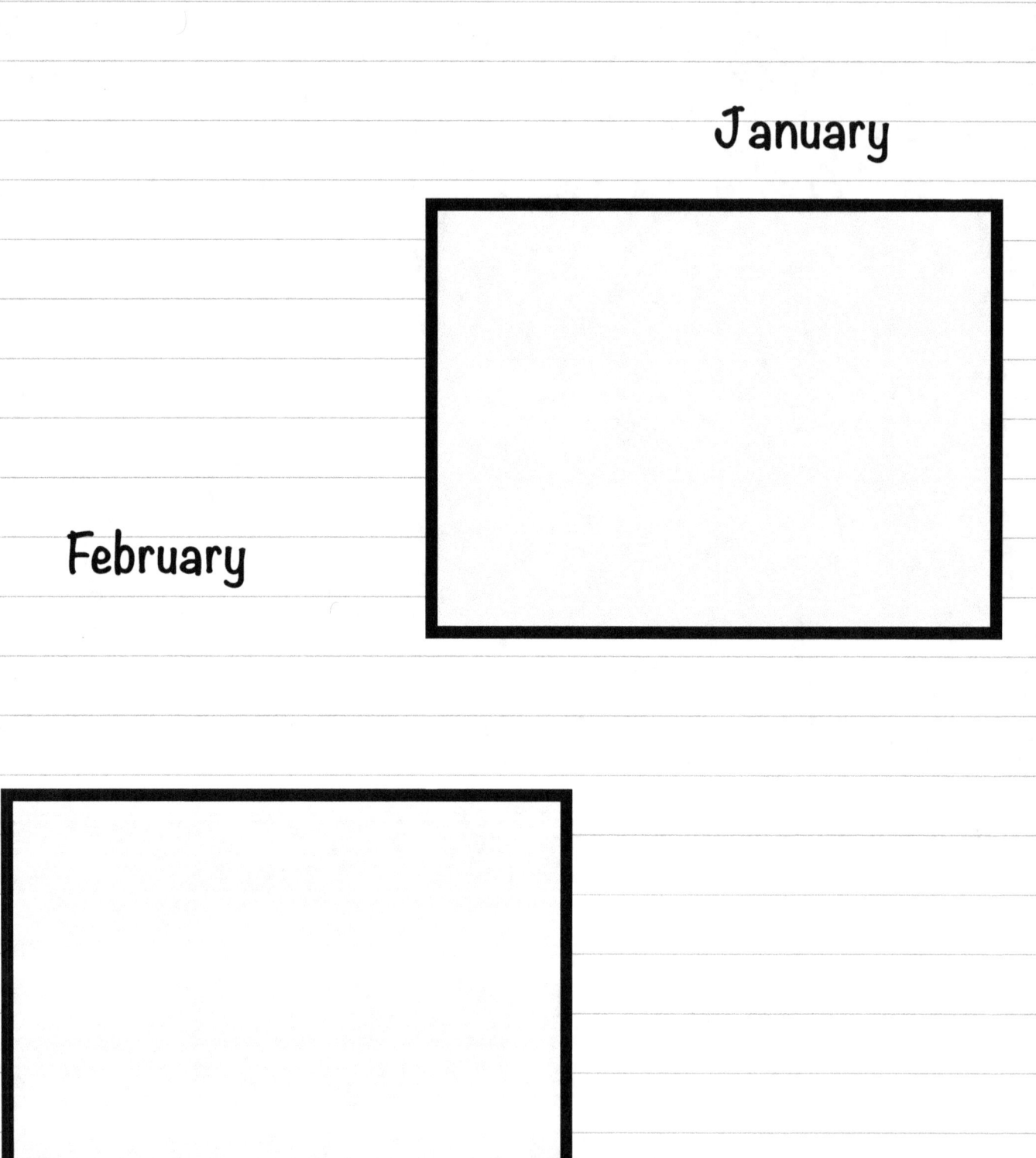

January

February

Your Accountability Journal
Monthly Snap Shots..

March

"Post pictures, phrases, words of memorable moments...."

Jada Williams

Monthly SnapShots..

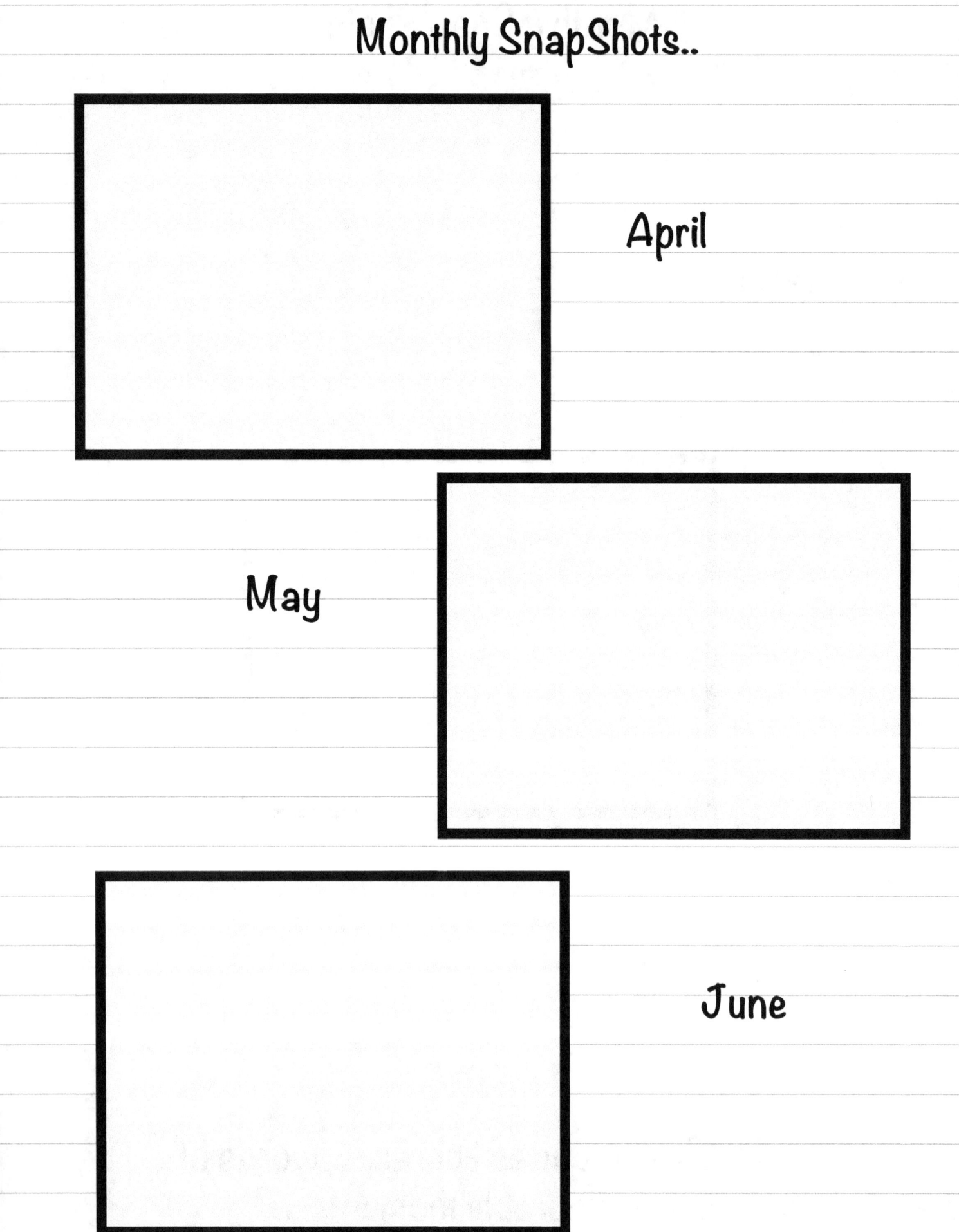

April

May

June

Monthly Snap Shots..

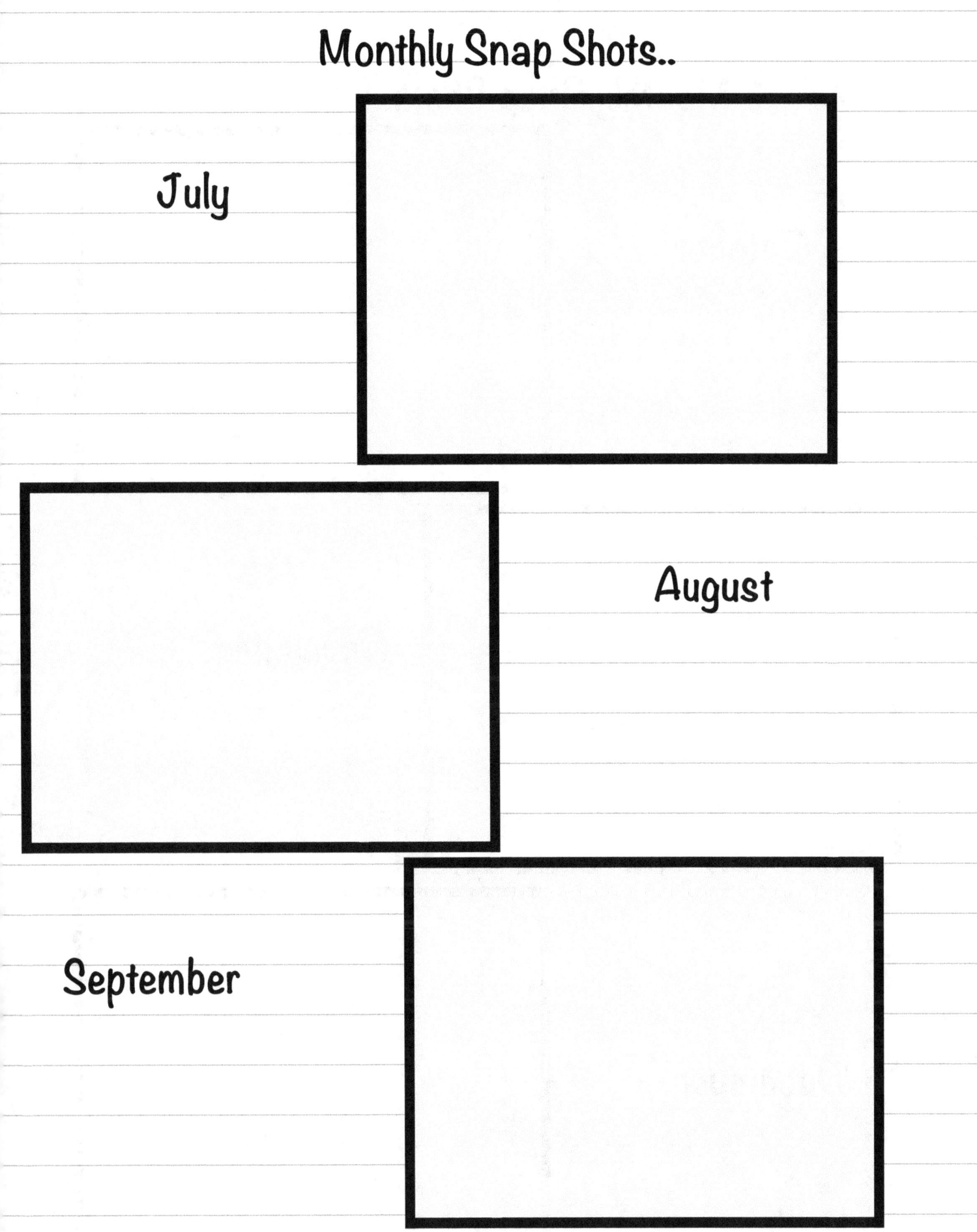

July

August

September

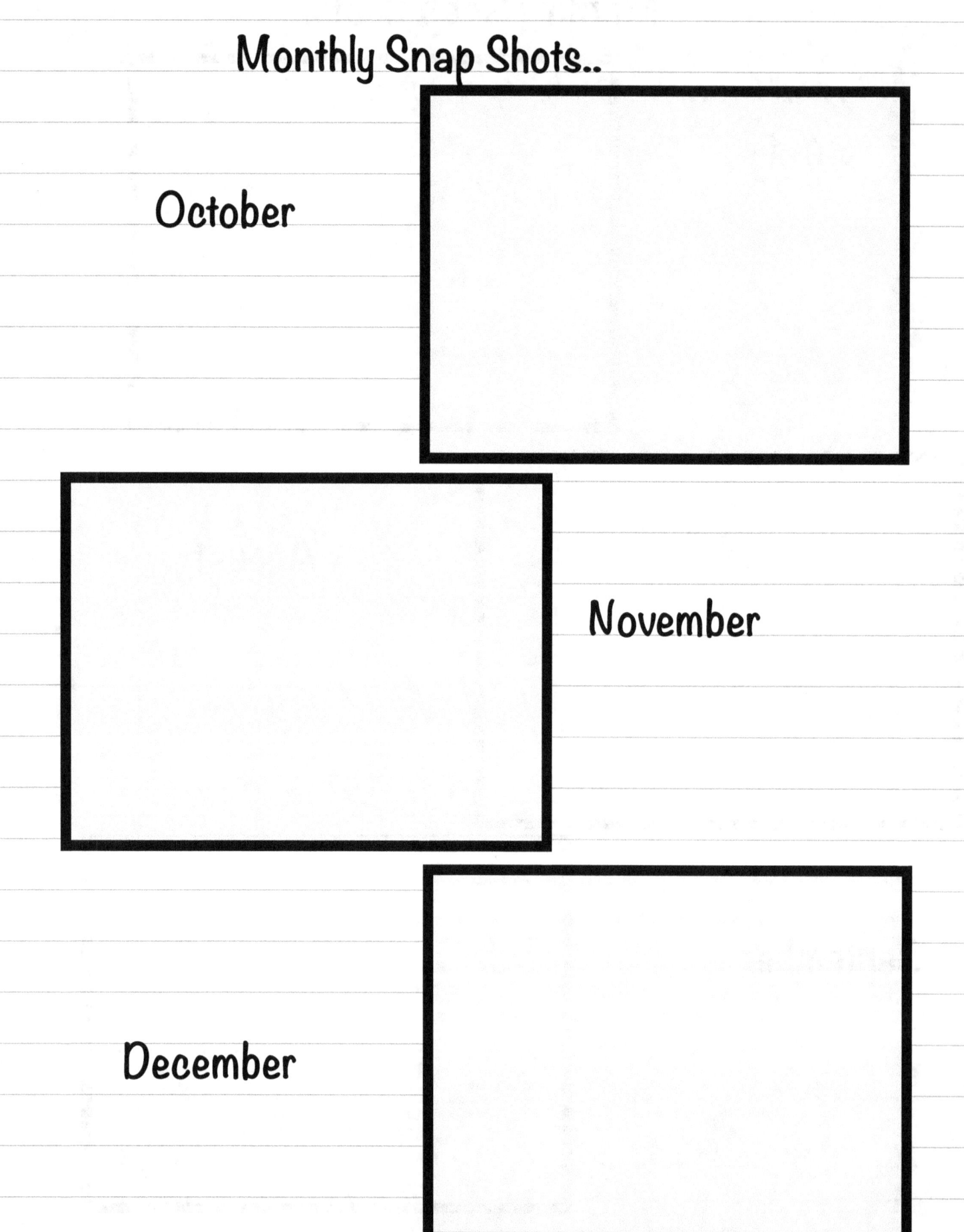

Vision Board

Highlights

Your Accountability Journal

Jada Williams

About the Author

Jada Williams

Jada Williams, as a little girl, told her mother that she would kiss the world and be an international business women. A graduate of Alabama A&M University, she received a Bachelor's of Science and a Business degree as a dual-sport scholarship recipient. Jada Williams was eager to start a professional career in the Logistics, supply chain management field.

Jada brings years of experience in logistics, business development, management and coaching from working with international companies. Out of these experiences she has embodied the name "Lady Logistics".

Jada believes in the core values of building relationships and developing business solutions that not only drive revenue for corporate sales, but also build people, build teams, and connect the dots providing solutions for foreign client business transactions that are transferable to your personal life experiences as well. Jada has spearhead consulting strategies for small start-up companies and has been the support to existing companies, helping them achieve their goals. She does not limit herself to the logistics industry. She has the ability to provide sound, business solutions across multiple industry verticals.

Jada decided as an educated, mother of two, to take the very talents she was naturally blessed with and the ones professionally trained by industry leaders in the market and build her own company Kis Ls Inc.. Today Jada Williams has built Kis Ls Inc. to be a business consulting firm providing solutions uniquely tailored for specific client needs. Jada credits her networking, the ability to coordinate, being detailed oriented and her unwavering focus for customer satisfaction as the catalyst for success in her new company. Through her new company Jada is looking forward to the opportunity to kiss the word with her proven business plan and experiences.

www.ingramcontent.com/pod-product-compliance
Lightning Source LLC
Chambersburg PA
CBHW081619100526
44590CB00021B/3515